Senate Foreign Relations Committee

Hearing on the Crisis in Egypt

July 25, 2013

Table of Contents

Senate Foreign Relations Committee

Hearing on the Crisis in Egypt

July 25, 2013

Opening Statements of Chairman Robert Menendez

WASHINGTON, DC – U.S. Sen. Robert Menendez, Chairman of the Senate Foreign Affairs Committee, delivered the below statement, as prepared for delivery, at today's hearing, "Crisis in Egypt."

The remarks follow:

"Thank you for joining us today for this timely hearing on the unfolding circumstances in Egypt. I want to thank Ambassador Dennis Ross, Dr. Michelle Dunn, and Ambassador Daniel Kurtzer for being here today. We look forward to their perspectives on the situation in Egypt and its ramifications for the region and for the United States.

The situation in Egypt has tremendous implications for the region and for the United States. Our response and our policy must be carefully calibrated to press for the democratic reforms that have been demanded by the Egyptian people and at the same time, support U.S. national security interests in the region.

These two goals are not at odds with one another, but do require a complex policy response that allows us to advocate for much needed democratic reforms while also advocating for our own security needs.

At the end of the day, our policy and our laws must be nuanced enough to allow for a response that reflects our interests. It is my view that terminating

U.S. assistance at this time could provoke a further crisis in Egypt that would not be to our benefit.

Having said that, the future of our relationship with Egypt, to a great extent, will be determined by our actions in the coming weeks. Whether we will have a stable and willing partner on crucial matters of security -- combating terrorism, trafficking of weapons and people into the Sinai, and support for peace in the Middle East -- is up to us both. Alternatively, we can stand aside during this crisis and just hope for the best. While all our choices are difficult at this time, in my view, abandoning Egypt would be a particularly poor policy choice.

But whatever policy we ultimately choose, during this period of upheaval in Egypt, it is critical that all parties exercise restraint, protests remain peaceful, and that violence is rejected.

The interim government should take those concerns to heart and, above all, ensure that the restoration of democracy be as transparent and inclusive as possible.

Steps that exacerbate the divide in Egyptian society, including the use of force against protestors, and arrests and harassment of pro-Morsi and of Muslim Brotherhood leaders serve only to deepen the chasm and forestall reconciliation.

The only way forward to a pluralistic, vibrant, and stable democracy lies in the inclusion of all political parties and groups.

Let me be clear, our support is not unconditional and unending. At the end of the day, Egyptian leaders and the Egyptian military must show that they are committed to an inclusive political process, credible democratic elections, and democratic governance that protects the rights of religious minorities and women.

On that subject, I am deeply concerned about the treatment of Coptic Christians, women, and Syrian refugees in a destabilized Egypt.

The military and police forces must assure the safety of Egypt's minority groups, which means preventing the beating and killing of Christians and sexual assaults on women.

I am also disturbed by reports of Egypt turning its back on refugees fleeing the ever-worsening conflict in Syria.

Egypt's military and interim government should provide safe haven for innocent civilians fleeing the brutality of the Assad regime.

I also hope that Egypt's security forces will be vigilant in the increasingly violent Sinai, where innocent Egyptians have been killed and terrorist groups have launched attacks against Israel.

Finally, Egypt's government must quickly overturn the recent convictions of 43 NGO workers – those sentences were a travesty of justice and must not stand. Their work to support the emergence of a strong, pluralistic democracy is needed now more than ever.

I am hopeful that our panelists will leave us with a better understanding of the situation, the prospects for a peaceful, democratic resolution, and the choices

that lie before us."

Senate Foreign Relations Committee

Hearing on the Crisis in Egypt

July 25, 2013

Testimony of Ambassador (Ret) Dr. Daniel C. Kurtzer

Current situation in Egypt

Egypt remains in a state of revolutionary upheaval, marked by political, economic, and social instability. Since the ouster of former President Hosni Mubarak in February 2011, Egypt's political parties and groupings have been beset by severe internal wrangling, and they remain badly fractured. Successive administrations have failed to establish security and basic law and order, and have also failed to secure enough political consensus from opposing political forces so as to be able to govern effectively.

Ousted President Mohamed Morsi faced, and could not resolve, pressing problems: a breakdown in law and order, especially acute in the Sinai Peninsula; depleted foreign exchange holdings, exacerbated by slowdowns in key economic sectors; and food and energy shortages. Morsi's own actions contributed to significant doubts about his and the Muslim Brotherhood's agenda, sparking fear of a rapid Islamicization of Egypt. He fired judges, paid little heed to violence against Coptic Christians, rammed through a new constitution, failed to take any steps to remedy the economic crisis, and seized nearly all powers in his own hands. Because the election to the People's Assembly (Parliament) had been nullified by the courts, no mechanism existed constitutionally to challenge Morsi's rule. In place of an unavailable impeachment process, a civil society organization, Tamarod, organized an unprecedented mass petition and mass rallies involving an estimated twenty million Egyptians throughout the country, representing all classes and social strata. This led the military to oust Morsi in early July and install an interim civilian-led administration.

The interim government is now in place, and it is the strongest and most reputable since 2011. The government is reaching out to the Muslim Brotherhood to try to launch a national reconciliation process, but the Brotherhood thus far is demanding conditions—such as the restoration to office of Morsi—that are unacceptable to both the government and the military. The government has also promised a rapid return to constitutional rule, including a process for amending and approving a revised constitutions and new elections for president and the parliament.

Viability of the interim government's roadmap to restore democratic government

The new Cabinet faces at least four daunting challenges: to stabilize the internal situation and restore law and order, thus providing a much needed sense of security for Egyptians to return to normal life; to find a pathway to political reconciliation with the Muslim Brotherhood, thus preventing a possible spiral of violence between supporters of the government and army and supporters of the Brotherhood; to kick-start the economy which has been stalled since the 2011 revolution, a task made easier by an injection of substantial Arab aid and loans; and to organize a fair, transparent process of amending the constitution and conducting new elections for president and parliament.

Of these urgent requirements, the most challenging will be the reintegration of the Muslim Brotherhood into the political process. Mutual distrust, the desire for settling scores, and long-term antipathy between the Brotherhood and the military complicate this process. The interim government reportedly has reached out to the Brotherhood, but the Brotherhood's preconditions--to restore Morsi to the presidency, reaffirm the constitution, and reinstate the Shura Council--have been a stumbling block, perhaps insurmountable. In the meantime, the

Brotherhood continues to mobilize demonstrations of its own, and it is surely capable to doing violent things.

In this standoff between the Brotherhood and the military, each counts on a strong base of support. The Brotherhood has long experience in maintaining its internal base, having spent much of its eighty-five years underground. But the Brotherhood has lost ground in the past year, and is now more hard-pressed to demonstrate the political clout that brought its leadership to power during the past two years.

On the other hand, it is widely accepted in Egypt since the 1952 revolution that the military is the most important symbol and embodiment of modern Egyptian nationalism. The liberal parties that flourished in Egypt before the 1952 revolution proved unable to govern, stand up to British domination, or deal with the corruption of the monarchy. For the past decades, the military has been content, in the words of Dr. Steven Cook, to "rule" but not "govern", that is, it sees itself as the ultimate arbiter of power in the country but does not want to govern day to day. Indeed, the military's poor governing performance after the 2011 revolution reinforced the preference to sit behind, rather than on, the seat of power.

It is possible, surely desirable, that this state of affairs change over time, as Egypt's very nascent democracy matures. For this change to happen, Egypt needs to develop more mature democratic institutions and a more tolerant democratic political culture and atmosphere. This is simply not the situation today.

Prospects for further political and civil unrest

Increasingly violent confrontations between the Muslim Brotherhood and the security forces, as well as the serious breakdown of law and order in the Sinai Peninsula, almost guarantee that things will remain unstable in Egypt for some time. Even if the interim government can induce the Brotherhood to enter reconciliation talks, the government will require a strong, coercive capacity to ensure domestic calm. Absent this, the violence could easily deteriorate over time into civil war.

In this respect, it would make no sense for the United States to cut off aid to the Egyptian military, the one group in Egypt that continues to share our interests and the only group ultimately capable of assuring domestic stability. The standing of the

United States in Egypt today is as low as it has been at any time since the days of Gamal Abdel Nasser. A cut-off of assistance now would gain nothing for the United States, but would surely alienate us from the military.

American national security interests in Egypt

The United States has important national security interests in Egypt:

- Military cooperation and coordination: Virtually everyone and everything the U.S. military sends to Afghanistan and the Gulf passes through or over Egypt, and Egyptian military coordination/cooperation is vital to the execution of our military's missions. The Egyptians provide vital, expedited Suez Canal clearances, and facilities for the repair and refueling of our planes and equipment.

- Intelligence cooperation: Egypt and the United States maintain a robust and mutually-beneficial intelligence relationship.

- Anti-terrorism cooperation: Egypt has been a significant partner in the United States effort to push back against global terrorism.

- Peace process: The Egyptian-Israeli peace treaty remains the cornerstone of efforts to achieve a comprehensive peace, and Egypt's support for Palestinian peacemaking efforts remains vital.

- Regional politics: While Egypt's leadership role in Arab and Muslim politics has softened in recent years, its influence remains in moderate politics in the region.

- Democratic change: Notwithstanding all the challenges noted above, Egypt's slow and unsteady march toward democracy continues to represent a very important model for the rest of the region, in either its possible success or failure.

Options for U.S. foreign policy to support the restoration of democracy, including the appropriate role of U.S. foreign assistance

There is a story, possibly apocryphal, of a Soviet general who was asked in 1972 whether the Soviets were upset about Sadat's decision to expel Soviet military advisers from Egypt. "Certainly," the general replied, "we are upset about losing our foothold in Egypt. But remember, we enjoyed 17 years of strategic friendship…not bad."

It is extremely hard for global actors to maintain a strategic relationship with regional states over a long period of time. Not only do their interests fail to align properly, but there are great incentives for both to play off the other in a constantly shifting environment of regional and global politics. The U.S.-Egyptian relationship is entering its forty-fifth year--a remarkable achievement in and of itself.

That said, no relationship can remain static in the face of changes in the environment. Although Egypt continues to face security challenges—Sinai, Ethiopia water, regional conflict spillover—a reasonable (non-professional) assessment is that Egypt could sustain a gradual, steady diminution in U.S. military assistance. Indeed, it would have made sense years ago to shift U.S. aid gradually from military to economic assistance; and it will make sense to do so in the future, after the domestic political and economic situation stabilizes. Today, however, Egypt's emergency economic and financial needs are acute. The successful conclusion of an IMF agreement should stimulate substantial external assistance, including from the United States; and, as noted above, it is vital to maintain our relationship with the military.

Morsi's ouster was not a preference of American policy, just as Morsi's actions while in office were not consistent with American interests. The reality is our bilateral relationship has changed, and the leverage and the influence the United States used to exercise in Egypt no longer are as potent. But in the same way that current events represent a second chance for the Egyptian revolution to succeed, they also represent a strategic opportunity for the United States to stabilize and strengthen our relationship with Egypt, and to preserve important American interests.

Senate Foreign Relations Committee

Hearing on the Crisis in Egypt

July 25, 2013

Testimony of Ambassador Dennis Ross, Counselor, the Washington Institute for Near East Policy

Good morning Chairman Menendez, Ranking Member Corker, and distinguished Committee members. I am pleased to appear before the Committee again. The last time I appeared was to address Syria and the challenges of the civil war— challenges that affect our interests morally and strategically. Today, I am here to talk about the recent events in Egypt. While the nature of the challenge and our choices for responding are fundamentally different, there should be no mistaking that both our values and strategic interests are also very much at stake.

Egypt is the largest Arab country; historically, its influence has been felt politically and culturally throughout the region. It has often been the trendsetter or bellwether, and today its direction is sure to affect the shape of the Middle East.

The Arab Awakening may have begun in Tunisia, but it was Tahrir Square that captured the imagination of the region and much of the world. And it is again the events in Tahrir Square and elsewhere on Egyptian streets that a new, unsettling reality in Egypt is being created. A democratically-elected leader was removed and is now under arrest. In Egypt itself, however, a majority seem to feel that this was the only possible option open to the Egyptian public. They saw a leader and his Muslim Brotherhood backers incapable of dealing with Egypt's problems and more focused on control than governance.

Though the claims may vary on how many people turned out on the streets of Cairo—with some estimates ranging as high as 13 to 14 million people—there is no disputing the fact that massive, unprecedented numbers of Egyptians demonstrated and called for the removal of a leadership that they saw leading their country to ruin. Many who had voted for President Morsi felt betrayed by his leadership that they saw as exclusionary, authoritarian, intolerant, and incompetent. The numbers that responded to the Tamarod (rebellion) petitions on recall, as well as to the call for demonstrations on June 30 to demand that Mohammad Morsi step down, are simply staggering. A critical mass of Egyptians signed the petition,s and the opposition embodied all classes and walks of life. No doubt the economic breakdown, the rise in prices, electricity black and brown outs, the gas and bread lines, the absence of law and order—and the seeming indifference and inability of the Morsi-led government to address these daily problems of life—triggered much of the opposition.

It is not an exaggeration to describe what happened on June 30 as a popular uprising against the Morsi-led government—a popular revolt that the military used to remove the Egyptian president and crack down on the leadership of the Muslim Brotherhood. For many in the Middle East, this second Egyptian revolution constitutes an important course correction. Certainly, that explains why Saudi Arabia, the UAE, and Kuwait have pledged over $12 billion of assistance to Egypt, and they have already begun delivering on that assistance.

Others challenge this narrative of a popular uprising that triggered military intervention and the replacement of the Morsi-led, Muslim Brotherhood dominated government. They see not a course correction, but a democratically elected government removed by the Egyptian military. This is certainly the argument of the Muslim Brotherhood and their supporters in Egypt, and they hope to gain international support for their demand that Morsi be reinstated. They say they will not rest until he is reinstated and threaten to disrupt life in Egypt until this happens.

The United States is not the central player in the drama that is being played out in Egypt today. But we are also not a bystander. For understandable reasons, we must be deeply troubled when a democratically elected leader is removed not at the ballot box but by the military. In addition, it is hard to escape the reality that Egypt today is deeply polarized between those who support the removal of the Morsi-led government and those who oppose what they call a coup and the new interim civilian government that has now been appointed. The prospect of bridging this divide in the near term is very small. Though there are rumors of mediation efforts between the Brotherhood and the military or those in the new interim government, it is hard to see an agreement any time soon. The Brotherhood insists on Morsi's reinstatement and the military absolutely rejects such a possibility.

Some hold out hope that a compromise may yet be possible; one in which Morsi would be reinstated for a brief symbolic time, would then step down in favor of a technocratic interim government, and new elections would then take place for president. In an atmosphere in which there were both bridge builders and a readiness on the part of the main protagonists—the military and the Brotherhood—to reach a compromise, it might be possible. But such an environment does not exist today and is not going to exist any time soon.

Instead, the military and security forces have cracked down on the leaders of the Brotherhood, arrested hundreds of their followers, and closed down their media outlets—and they have done so with support and applause from much of the Egyptian public, including from many, but not all, liberal voices. In addition, a new civilian interim government has been named with no Islamists in it. Moreover, 11 of the 34 members of the new cabinet served as ministers under Mubarak. The polarization is real. As much as we might inveigh against it, we should have no illusions that it is a temporary phenomenon.

The Muslim Brotherhood may speak of a coup and of democracy cheated. But in power, the Brotherhood did not act democratically. By appointing primarily members of the Brotherhood to key positions, issuing decrees to deny judicial oversight, pushing a law to remove 3000 judges, drafting a constitution only with Islamists, rushing through a referendum on that constitution, using its thugs to brutalize protestors outside the presidential palace, prosecuting those who insulted the president, and failing to address a collapsing economy, the Brotherhood alienated a majority of the Egyptian public. This is not just the "deep state" reacting. This is not just a return of the *"feloul"* —or Mubarak apparatchiks—resuming control.

The interim cabinet led by Prime Minister Hazam El-Beblawi has a number of highly credible figures in it who don't represent the so-called deep state. Beblawi, himself, is a well-respected economist.

Similarly, two of the deputy prime ministers, Hossam Eissa and Ziad Bahaa El-Din are genuine liberals, one a co-founder of the Constitution Party and the other a founding member of the Social Democratic Party. The Minister of Finance, Ahmed Galal, spent 18 years at the World Bank—and there are others whose background and experience qualify them as genuine technocrats. But, as noted above, there are also those who were part of the era of Mubarak governance. And General El-Sissi is not only the Defense Minister and Commander of the Military, he is also one of the deputy prime ministers—something that adds to the suspicion that the military, for all its talk of not wanting to govern, is the force behind all decision-making.

At this point, there can be little doubt that the military is the key arbiter of events in Egypt. The question for us is what to do now. The last thing the United States wants to see is for Egypt to become a failed or failing state. Certainly, we would like to see Egypt proceed on a path that promotes a representative, inclusive, tolerant government that tackles its problems and respects minority and women's rights and fulfills its international obligations, including its peace treaty with Israel. The challenge for us is to adopt policies, recognizing the limits of our influence, that still offer more of a chance to see Egypt move in that direction.

Some argue that we should cut off assistance to Egypt. They say there was a coup; our law requires a cut-off; our principles demand it; and for the sake of consistency and credibility we should act accordingly. I respect this position but disagree with it. I don't do so easily. But I do so because I fear, at least at this juncture, that cutting off assistance would mean losing whatever leverage and influence we might be able to employ in Egypt today. Presently, the military is the most important actor in Egypt, and we must take into account that it has extensive public support.

The moment we cut off assistance, we not only will trigger a backlash from the military but also from a wide segment of the Egyptian public. We will be seen as trying to dictate to Egypt against the will of the people. Our claims of simply following our laws and our principles may ring true here but will not in Egypt. Nor will they have much resonance elsewhere in the region where the preoccupation remains largely centered on Syria and where the widely held perception is that America's principles don't seem to be guiding us there.

Furthermore, we should have no illusions: the Saudis and Emirates will be quick to fill in for lost American assistance at least in the near term. And while we may be focused on getting the Egyptian military and its new civilian government to exercise restraint and to be inclusive, the Saudis and Emirates will urge just the opposite. They see the Muslim Brotherhood and the rise of political Islam as a mortal threat and believe they must be suppressed—not included or treated as legitimate political participants.

In arguing against a cut-off of assistance, I am, at the same time, also arguing that we must use our leverage. Without exaggerating our leverage, it is fair to say we have some. The Egyptian military surely does not want us to cut our assistance in part because they have become dependent on US weapons and a broad support structure—something that is in our mutual interests. But beyond wanting to avoid the practical consequences of seeing pipelines potentially cut and material supplies put on hold, the military also does not want us to lend credence to the Brotherhood's narrative of a coup. That would surely will hurt Egypt's standing internationally—making meaningful assistance from others outside of the region far more difficult to obtain.

The real issue, therefore, is how to try to use our leverage and to what ends. Here I would focus on:

- Trying to get the military to truly go back to the barracks;

- Acting with restraint and minimizing their own use of violence;

- Ensuring that the interim government is empowered to make decisions and deal with real problems—and that means as an example not deferring discussions with the IMF but actually concluding them;

- Having the transition process be transparent;

- Emphasizing that only those who advocate violence would be excluded from the political process and elections;

- Committing to having international monitors come in to observe the elections, even if that requires less haste and more preparation for those elections;

- And, lastly, demonstrating a clear commitment to building civil society and its institutions.

This last point is critical. One of the clearest signs that the military and the interim government are serious about building a fair and open society and advancing the cause of representative government would be to pardon those representatives of those civil society groups who were found guilty of violating Egyptian laws. The military and interim government should act to revoke those laws and support the drafting of new ones that would permit NGOs to operate freely and effectively with financial support from inside and outside. If there are to be repeatable elections that are fairly contested and more likely to be respected—and a real space opened up for political pluralism— Egypt must build the institutions of civil society. We should use our leverage to press for this.

We should also press to permit the Muslim Brotherhood to participate in elections—assuming they are not encouraging their supporters to engage in violence. If they choose not to participate, let that be their decision.

None of this will happen easily, and there are no guarantees that even if we seek to use our leverage we will succeed. But cutting off the assistance now won't end up serving our interests or our values. Egypt's political future is bound to be messy and to move in fits and starts. We should try to use our leverage quietly for now, but there should be no doubt on the part of the military and the interim government that we will become more vocal and if there is no responsiveness, we will be prepared to cut off assistance.

I don't reject cutting off assistance or reshaping it in principle. I reject it now because I think it will backfire and not serve our hopes and aims for how Egypt should evolve. Our stakes in Egypt remain high. It makes sense for us to stay in the game and try to affect Egypt's course, and not make a statement that will render us largely irrelevant as Egyptians shape an uncertain future.

Senate Foreign Relations Committee

Hearing on the Crisis in Egypt

July 25, 2013

Testimony of Michele Dunne, Vice President, Director, Rafik Hariri Center for the Middle East Atlantic Council

Chairman Menendez, Ranking Member Corker, members of the Committee, thank you for the honor of testifying before this committee about the crisis in Egypt. As we analyze the political turmoil in Egypt and try to sort out US policy options, I would like to raise four points for your consideration:

First, the July 3 removal of Muslim Brotherhood President Mohammed Morsi by military coup following enormous demonstrations should not be understood primarily as a triumph of secularism over Islamism. Along with secularists and Islamists, there is a third major player in Egyptian politics: the state itself, which was left largely intact after the removal of former President Hosni Mubarak in February 2011. In the period after Mubarak's ouster, the military (the most powerful player within the state) worked with the Islamists and against the secular opposition. Now the military, as well as other state institutions that were on the defense after the 2011 revolution, have allied with the secular parties against the Brotherhood. So what has happened is in part a reassertion of the Mubarak era state, a sort of counterrevolution.

In addition, it is important to recognize that the current state-secularist alliance is anti-Brotherhood but not necessarily anti-Islamist. The Salafi Nour Party supported the removal of Morsi and has already exerted its influence by vetoing cabinet choices and getting its preferred wording on the status of Islamic sharia into the temporary constitution.

Second, the United States should reserve judgment for now as to whether the removal of Morsi will put Egypt back on a path toward democracy or not. It is too soon to tell and the signs are contradictory. On the positive side of the ledger, the military is not exerting control directly but rather has put civilians out front, including a president from the judiciary and a cabinet including respected technocrats and well known secular political figures. The cabinet is particularly well placed to address the economy, which is in dire straits. And the new transition roadmap puts the rewriting of the constitution before the holding of new parliamentary and presidential elections. This corrects a major flaw of the first transition in which constitution writing followed elections, allowing the winners to dominate the process and exclude the losers.

On the negative side of the ledger, the way in which the democratic process was cast aside on July 3 is troubling. Morsi was a failure as a president, who behaved as though winning 52 percent of the vote gave him a mandate to rule as a pharaoh. The broad public opposition to his leadership was real, seen in the millions who signed a petition for early elections and poured into the streets on June 30. But it would have been much more powerful and salutary for

Egypt's young democracy if Morsi had been defeated in an early election or referendum; instead, his removal from office by the military shortly after protests began sets a dangerous precedent. Instead of learning the lesson that ineffective and undemocratic governance brings a comeuppance at the ballot box, the Brotherhood and others Islamists have learned that playing the democratic game by the rules does not pay off.

In addition, the new transition is in danger of repeating the most important mistake of the earlier post-Mubarak stage, which was a failure to build a broad consensus because critical players were excluded from important decisions. Before the July 3 removal of Morsi it was the secular liberals and leftists who were excluded; now it is the Muslim

Brotherhood. Egypt is moving into a period in which one of the most deeply-rooted movements in the country's political life might be excluded, perhaps severely repressed or at a minimum strongly disadvantaged, just as the secularists were until recently.

While Egyptian officials are speaking the language of inclusion and reconciliation, their actions toward the Muslim Brotherhood are saying the opposite. In addition to Mohammed Morsi, an undisclosed number—perhaps two dozen—of senior leaders of the Brotherhood and its Freedom and Justice Party are detained incommunicado without charge, with new rumors surfacing daily about serious crimes with which they might be charged, including treason. They have been banned from travel and their assets seized. The Brotherhood-dominated upper house of parliament has been dissolved, and the new transition government is busy expunging Brotherhood appointees from bodies such as the Supreme Press Council and National Council for Human Rights. And there is talk of outlawing the Brotherhood itself, which only recently gained license as a non-governmental organization.

Third, despite the military's argument that it spared the country a civil war, Egypt might well be headed into greater instability. The new transition might once again produce a constitution and elected bodies that a significant part of the population considers illegitimate, leading to repeated political breakdowns, resets, and military intervention in politics—a cycle of instability. Already there has been a troubling spike in violence, with more than 160 killed and 1400 injured in demonstrations, daily clashes between pro and anti-Morsi groups throughout the country, and hundreds arrested. Jihadi attacks against military and police officers in the Sinai have increased sharply, with more than 20 officers killed in the past two weeks. With Islamists rethinking the value of peaceful political participation, Egypt could easily see a return to the type of insurgency and domestic terrorism it experienced in the 1990s, when jihadis targeted government officials, Christians, and tourists. Under those circumstances, it will not be possible to attract tourists and investment back to Egypt in the numbers needed to revitalize the economy.

Fourth, in light of these many dangers, the United States should proceed with caution and be guided by basic principles. Egypt can only be a reliable security partner for the United States and peace partner for Israel if it is reasonably stable, and it will only become stable once it develops a governing system that answers strong popular demands for responsiveness, accountability, fairness, and respect for citizens' rights.

There will be signs in the coming weeks showing in which direction Egypt is moving after this cataclysmic change. Will Morsi and other Brotherhood leaders be released and encouraged to participate in peaceful politics, or will they be imprisoned on trumped-up charges? Will there be freedom for the media, including those affiliated with the Brotherhood? Will the process to amend the constitution be broadly inclusive, or will it be rushed, non-transparent, and designed to meet the demands of a chosen few, such as the military and the Salafis? Will Egyptian and foreign non-governmental organizations be given freedom to operate and serve as watchdogs of the transition, and will the recent convictions of 43 NGO workers (including 16 Americans) be reversed?

The United States should take this time to pause, suspend military deliveries and assistance in accordance with our law, and review policy towards and assistance to Egypt, including special privileges such as cash flow financing for Foreign Military Financing. The US administration should carry out its own internal review as well as a broad dialogue with

Egyptians inside and outside the government, with the stated intention of resuming assistance as soon as the country is clearly back on a democratic path. Military and economic assistance should not be kept on autopilot as they were during the Mubarak years, but updated in order to support a stable, prosperous, democratic Egypt that plays a vital and responsible role in the Middle East region.

The United States is understandably wary of damaging its longstanding relationship with the Egyptian government and military, but it should also avoid pursuing a policy that appears cynical and unprincipled. Hewing too closely to the party currently in power, treating opposition groups and civil society as irrelevant, and ignoring democratic principles have earned the United States sharp criticism from all sides in Egypt. But we should not make the mistake of concluding that the United States no longer has any influence there; the fact that Egyptians still pay such close attention to what our officials and diplomats do and say suggests quite the opposite.